A Tha

MW00886350

I want to say Thank You for buying my book so I put together a free gift for you!

This gift is the perfect complement to this book so just hit the link below to get access.

Click Here to Download Your Free Gift.

Contents

Introduction

Welcome to "The Hot Sauce Book" thank you for buying.

Do you love hot sauces? Well, this is the book for you.

A book full of recipes for easily whipping up your own delicious signature sauces to impress your family and friends. Get ready to set their palates ablaze.

I love to cook with spices and hot sauces, but up until a few years ago I always used store bought sauces. That all changed when I got new neighbors.

A new couple moved in next door to us and we were invited round for dinner, and what a dinner it was. It turned out that Adriana and Macro have roots in Ecuador and, wow did their cooking reflect that.

It was absolutely amazing with the star of the show being the homemade signature sauces that Adriana had made.

Meeting Adriana and Marco was the genesis for my journey into the world of spices and homemade signature hot sauces. Over the next years Adriana and I became fast friends and I absorbed all her knowledge on how to make amazingly simple and delicious hot sauces.

This book is the collection of the most delicious signature sauce recipes I have, as well as a whole host recipes influenced by the sauces for breakfast, lunch and dinner.

So get ready to learn the techniques behind making your own signature sauces that will wow your friends and family.

In this book I show you how to make sauces ranging from mild to "blow your head off hot" as well as fruity inspired sauces, alcohol infused sauces and garlic sauces.

Every recipe in this book has been kept as simple as possible. You won't find any difficult steps or uncommon terms.

So get out the peppers, spices and pans because we are going to dive into the world of homemade signature hot sauces.

Happy cooking.

Lots of love,

Sarah Sophia

The Sauces

Ingredients
Spice Level: Hot

½ pound of tomatillos, husked
⅓ cup of finely chopped cilantro
3 serrano peppers, stems removed and roughly chopped
1 onion, chopped finely
1 tablespoon garlic, minced
The juice from 1 lime
1 tablespoon apple cider vinegar
Salt, to taste

Directions

Take a medium pot add the tomatillos and cover water. Heat over high heat.

When the water is boiled, remove from the heat and set aside to rest until they darken slightly. This will take around 5 minutes, after this drain the tomatillos.

Add tomatillos to your blender. Pulse until a coarse purée is formed.

Add the cilantro, peppers, garlic, onion, lime juice, and vinegar to blender and pulse for 10 to 15 seconds.

Salt to taste and stir in well.

Store in a lidded jar or empty bottle.

Ingredients
Spice Level: Hot

¼ cup long red hot peppers, stems removed, sliced thinly
3 tablespoons red Thai chillies, stems and seeds removed,
sliced thinly
2 tablespoons garlic, minced
2 tablespoons rice vinegar
1 tablespoon tomato paste
½ tablespoons sugar
2 tablespoons fish sauce
2 tablespoons oil, canola oil is best
1.5 tablespoons water

Directions

Prepare the ingredients as stated above.

Take your blender and add all the ingredients. Except for the
water.

Pulse until smooth.

Taste the sauce and season with salt to your taste. Add the
water.

Blend again for 5 seconds.

Ingredients
Spice Level: Very Hot

1 tablespoon olive oil
1 cup of roughly chopped carrots
½ cup finely sliced onion
4 garlic cloves, minced
5 habanero peppers
¼ cup water
¼ cup of juice from squeezed lime
¼ cup white vinegar
1 medium - large tomato
Salt and black pepper to taste

Directions

In a pan add the oil and place over a medium heat.

Add the carrots, onion, garlic and cook for 5 minutes. Ensure you still well whilst cooking.

Take a blender and add the contents of the pan, as well as adding the peppers, water, lime juice, vinegar and the tomato. Blend until smooth.

Taste and season with salt and black pepper to taste.

Transfer to the pan from step one and cook for 3 minutes on a medium heat.

Store in jar or empty bottle.

Roasted Tomatillo & Jalapeno Salsa Verde

Ingredients
Spice Level: Medium

4 tomatillos, husked
1 jalapeno, stem removed
1 clove garlic, chopped
2 tablespoons of olive oil
1 pinch of cumin
Juice of 1 lime
1 bunch cilantro
Salt to taste

Directions

Preheat oven to 450F.

Take a baking tray, line with baking paper and add the tomatillos, jalapeno and garlic. Drizzle the olive oil or the top.

Cook for 15 minutes, ensure you turn once.

Add to a blender, along with any remaining oil and liquid on the baking paper. Throw in the cumin, lime juice, cilantro and salt (to taste) and blend for 25 seconds.

Store in jar or empty bottle.

Ingredients
Spice Level: Medium

8 red chilies, large
2 scotch bonnet peppers
4 cloves of garlic, separated and wrapped in foil
1 teaspoon smoked paprika
1 teaspoon sea salt
2 sprigs thyme
Vinegar
2 lemons, juiced

Directions

Preheat the oven to 400F.

On an oiled baking tray place the chillies and the foil wrapped garlic. Keep in oven for about 20-25 minutes, the chillies should be blackened and blistering.

Remove from oven and let them cool slightly. When cooled de-stem the chillies and chop finely. Remove the seeds from one of the bonnet peppers (unless you like it very hot)

Take the garlic from the foil and remove their skin.

Take your blender, or hand mixer and blend the peppers, garlic, paprika, salt and thyme until they form a puree. Add lemon juice and 1.5 tablespoon vinegar. Blend again for 5 seconds.

Store in jar or empty bottle.

Homemade Tabasco Sauce

Ingredients
Spice Level: Hot

20 tabasco chilies, stems removed
½ tablespoons minced garlic
1 small onion finely sliced
¾ teaspoon salt
1 teaspoon vegetable oil
2 cups water
1 cup distilled white vinegar

Directions

Place a pan over a high heat and add olive oil. Add the garlic, peppers and onion, sauté over 5 minutes or until the onion is translucent.

Add the salt and the water, continue to cook for 15 minutes, stirring occasionally. Peppers should be soft and the liquid should mostly have evaporated.

Take off the heat and allow to cool for 30 minutes.

Add to a food processor and puree until smooth.

Add the vinegar and blend for 5 seconds.

Season to taste with more salt, if necessary.

Strain through a mixture through a fine mesh sieve.

Store in a secure jar or bottle, with airtight lid for at least 2 weeks.

Note: this can be stored for up to 6 months in a refrigerator.

Ingredients
Spice Level: Mild

1 cup mayonnaise
½ oz. Dijon mustard
½ oz. fresh squeezed lime juice
1 oz. chipotle chili in adobo, pureed
¼ oz. fresh garlic, minced
Salt, to taste

Directions

In a mixing bowl combine all the ingredients and mix well. Use a hand blender if you prefer a thinner sauce.

Taste and season with more salt to taste.

Must be stored covered in the refrigerator.

Ingredients
Spice Level: Hot

2 tablespoons oil
1 white onion, finely chopped
2 cloves garlic, finely chopped or minced
2 ripe mangoes, skinned, pitted and coarsely chopped
1 habanero chili, chopped finely
3 tablespoons honey
1 cup white wine vinegar
Salt, to taste

Directions

Place a pan over a medium heat and add oil. Once the oil is heated add the onions and garlic and cook for 3 minutes.

Add the mango and habanero, continue to cook for 5 minutes, stirring frequently.

Add the honey and vinegar, turn heat to low and cook for 12 minutes.

Transfer everything to a blender and pulse until smooth. If mixture is too thick add 2 tablespoons of warm water.

Strain the mixture through a fine-mesh sieve. Season with salt to taste.

Ingredients
Spice Level: Hot

2 tablespoons olive oil
1 large onion diced
2 medium chilli peppers, use your favourite peppers, stems removed
3 habanero peppers, stems removed
4 garlic cloves, minced
1 lb. of tomatoes, diced
1 cup distilled white vinegar
2 teaspoons salt
2 teaspoons sugar

Directions

In a large pan add oil and heat over a medium heat.

Add the onion, peppers, habaneros and garlic, cook for 5 minutes, stirring occasionally.

Reduce the heat to medium and add tomatoes, vinegar, salt and sugar. Cook, stirring occasionally, for 5 minutes.

Pour the contents of the pan into a food processor and blend until smooth.

Strain the contents, using a fine mesh sieve, over a medium bowl and push out all the solids to extract all the liquid. Throw away the solids and let the sauce cool to room temperature.

Ingredients
Spice Level: Mild

2 cups ketchup
6 cloves of garlic, crushed and peeled
1 cup water
2 tablespoons home-made hot sauce
¼ cup honey
2 tablespoons molasses
2 tablespoons brown sugar
1 teaspoon Worcestershire sauce
1 teaspoon soy sauce
1 teaspoon salt
2 tablespoons Cajun seasoning
1 pinch paprika
1 pinch crushed red pepper
1 pinch ground white pepper
1 pinch ground black pepper
2 tablespoons corn-starch
1 tablespoon water
½ cup butter

Directions

Take a large saucepan and place over a low heat. Add a splash of oil.

Add the ketchup, garlic, hot sauce, sugar, molasses, honey, Worcestershire sauce, soy sauce, salt (to taste), Cajun, paprika, red pepper, white pepper, black pepper and 1 cup of water to the pan and mix well.

Increase the heat to medium and bring to a simmer. When a simmer is reached turn the heat to low and let simmer for 20-25 minutes. Stir occasionally.

Take a bowl and add 1 tablespoon of water, dissolve the corn-starch in this. If more water is needed add 1 tablespoon at a time.

Add the now dissolved corn-starch to the sauce in the pan and stir well, continue to simmer for 10-15 minutes.

Stir butter into the sauce and simmer for 10 more minutes until the sauce begins to thicken.

Serve hot or cover and chill for use later.

Ingredients
Spice Level: Medium

1 cup water
2 tablespoons vinegar
1 habanero pepper, stems and seeds removed, roughly chopped
2 chipotle peppers in adobo sauce, roughly chopped
½ onion, finely diced
1 carrot, diced
¼ cup whiskey
Juice of one lemon
½ cup molasses
¼ teaspoon ground cumin
1 tablespoon sea salt

Directions

Place a pan over a medium heat and the water and vinegar.

After 30 seconds add the peppers, onion and carrot. Bring to a simmer before covering and simmering on low for 15 minutes.

Add the remaining ingredients and simmer for 3 minutes.

Let the mixture cool and then add to a food processor and puree.

Store in the refrigerator.

Peppered Steak Sauce

Ingredients
Hot Sauce: Medium

6 teaspoons green pepper
4 teaspoons black peppercorns
4 cups vegetable stock
1.5 cups white wine vinegar
15 capers
4 onions, chopped
40 grams dried shiitake mushrooms
6 green Cayenne pepper, de-stemmed and finely chopped
1 teaspoon garlic paste

Directions

In a large pot add ⅓ of the vegetable stock and bring to a boil.

Add the chopped onion to the stock and cook for 15 minutes.

Add the remaining stock to the pot. Once it starts to boil add the remaining ingredients except for the vinegar.

Take off the heat, cover and let rest for 60 minutes.

After the 60 minutes pour into a blender and pulse well.

Return to the pot and add the white wine vinegar. Bring to the boil. Cover and let cook for 20 minutes. Stirring occasionally.

If the sauce is too runny after the 20 minutes, let simmer with the lid off until it thickens.

Bottle and keep refrigerator.

Ingredients
Spice Level: Hot

10 habanero chili peppers, de-seeded and chopped finely
6 small ripe plums, roughly chopped
200ml malt vinegar
1 tomato, roughly chopped
8 teaspoons sesame seed oil
4 teaspoons brown sugar
3 teaspoons ginger paste
2 teaspoons cayenne pepper
1 teaspoon black mustard seeds
Juice of one lime
2 star anise pods
6 cloves of garlic, skin removed
½ tablespoon orange grated rind

Directions

Place a pot over a low heat and add the sesame oil. Add the star anise, garlic and mustard seeds. Stir well

Once the oil starts to boil add the ginger paste and stir. After 30 seconds add the brown sugar and stir well.

Cook for 2 minutes before adding the tomatoes and cayenne. Stir well.

Add the remaining ingredients, stir for 30 seconds. Increase heat so the pot is simmering.

Cover and cook for 20 minutes.

Remove the anise pods and garlic cloves after 20 minutes. They should be floating near, or close, to the top

Take off the heat and pour into a blender. Blend until smooth.

Return to the pot and cook for a further 10 minutes.

Meat Speciality Sauce

Ingredients
Spice Level: Mild

1 tablespoon bacon drippings, store bought or home-made
1 small, very finely chopped onion, or minced
1 tablespoon minced garlic
1 tablespoon minced ginger
½ cup ketchup
¼ cup Worcestershire sauce
¼ cup soy sauce
1 cup brown sugar, packed down firmly with back of spoon
1 cup balsamic vinegar
¼ cup fresh lemon juice
1 teaspoon chipotle sauce, store bought is fine
2 tablespoons ground mustard or powder
½ teaspoon chili pepper flakes
1 teaspoon ground black pepper
⅛ teaspoon salt
½ teaspoon ground powder
1 teaspoon coriander powder
½ teaspoon paprika

Directions

Put a pan over a medium heat and add the bacon drippings.

Add the onion and cook in the bacon drippings for 5 minutes. At this point add the garlic and ginger, cook for 1 minute, before lowering to a low heat.

In a small bowl add the ketchup, Worcestershire, soy sauce, sugar, balsamic vinegar, lemon juice, chipotle, mustard, chili pepper, pepper, salt, cumin, coriander, paprika and stir well.

Add to the pan, increase heat to medium and cook for 12-15 minutes stirring frequently.

Serve hot or cover and chill for use later.

Rum & Pineapple Sauce

Ingredients
Spice Level: Medium

2 tablespoons corn-starch
2 teaspoons dark rum
2 tablespoons soy sauce
1 teaspoon grated orange skin
1 tablespoon honey
1 20 oz. can crushed pineapple, drained but reserve the juice
2 habanero peppers, seeds and stems removed

Directions

Place a pan over a medium heat. Add 3 tablespoons of the pineapple juice, the peppers and the corn-starch.

Mix well before adding the remaining ingredients (including the rest of the pineapple juice) and mix again.

Bring to the boil stirring constantly.

Let cool and then pulse with a hand blender to remove any lumps from the crushed pineapple.

An Ale Sauce

Ingredients
Spice Level: Medium

2 tablespoons olive oil
5 red jalapenos, stems removed, chopped finely
2 serrano chilies, stems removed, chopped finely
5 cloves of garlic, minced or chopped finely
12 oz. ale
½ teaspoon smoked paprika
½ teaspoon salt
1 tablespoon rice wine vinegar
½ teaspoon white sugar

Directions

Place a pan coated with oil over a medium heat.

Add the jalapenos and chilies and cook for 5 minutes. Stirring frequently, they should be well softened after this time.

Add the garlic and cook for 30 seconds mixing well.

Pour in the beer and stir well. Add the remaining ingredients.

Bring to a simmer and leave for 6-8 minutes. Stir occasionally.

Take off the heat and allow to cool before pouring into a food blender.

Pulse until smooth.

Store in the refrigerator in an airtight container.

Ingredients
Spice Level: Mild

1 cup ketchup
½ cup blackberry preserves
¼ cup bourbon
2 small green onions, chopped finely, or minced
2 tablespoons red wine vinegar
1.5 tablespoons minced garlic
1 teaspoon Worcestershire sauce
1 teaspoon yellow mustard
Salt to taste

Directions

Take a medium mixing bowl and add all ingredients together. Mix well.

Transfer to a blender and pulse for 15 seconds.

Serve hot by heating in an oiled pot or cover and chill for use later.

Scotch Bonnet Hot Sauce

Ingredients
Spice Level: Very Hot

1 teaspoon vegetable oil
20 Scotch Bonnet peppers, chopped, stems and seeds removed
6 jalapeno peppers, chopped
6 cloves garlic, chopped or minced
½ cup minced, or finely sliced, onion
Pinch of salt, and more to taste
2 cups water
¼ cup distilled white vinegar
2 tablespoons white sugar

Directions

Put a pan over a medium heat and add oil, peppers, garlic, onion, and salt. Cook for 5 minutes, stirring frequently.

Add the water and continue to cook for 18-20 minutes. Stir frequently. The ingredients should all be soft by the end.

Take off the heat, set aside and allow to cool for 30 minutes.

Pour into a blender, and puree until smooth.

Add the vinegar and sugar; blend for another 20 seconds.

Keep refrigerated in airtight container. .

Sweet Hot Thai Chilli Sauce

Ingredients
Spice Level: Medium

2 cup brown sugar
1 cup white vinegar
1 cup water
3.5 tablespoons chopped or minced garlic
1.5 teaspoon salt
1.5 cup pureed red chilies

Directions

Place a pan over a medium heat and add the sugar, vinegar, water, garlic and salt. Mix well and bring to the boil.

Once boiled, turn heat to low, let simmer for 10 minutes.

Take off the heat and set aside. As it cools a syrup should form.
How to Make Pureed Chilies.

Take 4 cups of dried chillies and remove stems.

Add to a bowl and pour in boiling water, enough to cover the chilies. Stir for 5 minutes until they are softened,

Put the softened chilies in a blender and pulse for around 30 seconds.

They should now resemble a paste, if the mixture is too thick add 2 tablespoon of water and blend for 5 seconds.

Take paste from the blender add to the now cooled syrup and stir in well.

Store in a secure jar or bottle.

Ginger Beer Hot Sauce

Ingredients
Spice Level: Mild

120g mix of your favourite chilies, stems removed, chopped roughly
30g chilli flakes, dried
130g brown sugar
2 cups white wine vinegar
4 cloves chopped garlic
½ cup olive oil
1.5 cups ginger beer
Mint leaves, a handful, chopped
Half a lemon

Directions

Take a large saucepan, place over a medium heat. Add the chilies, sugar, lemon, vinegar and bring to the boil.

Turn heat down and leave simmering for 20 minutes.

Strain the liquid over a bowl with a fine mesh sieve. Throw the lemon half away.

Add the strained mixture to a blender along with 3 tablespoons of the liquid. Blend until a thick pulp forms.

Place the pan back over the heat and add the olive oil. Once heated add the pulped chilli mixture and fry for 30 seconds.

Add the remaining ingredients and to leave to simmer until it's thickened into a sauce.

Once this stage is reached, take off the heat and add the mint leaves to infuse. Stir well.

Roasted Pepita Sauce

Ingredients
Spice Level: Medium

2 cups pumpkin seeds
1 cup red wine vinegar
1 teaspoon salt
¼ chili powder, ancho is best
1 teaspoon garlic powder
1 tablespoon olive oil
½ teaspoon cayenne powder
1 tablespoon chipotle chili powder
3 cups water

Directions

Preheat oven to 350F.

Add a sheet of baking paper to a tray and place pumpkin seeds on them.

Cook in oven for 20 minutes. Shake the pan frequently to ensure cooked on each side and prevent burning. They should be toasted not burnt.

Remove from the oven and let cool for 15 minutes.
Add seeds and all the other ingredients to a blender and pulse until very smooth.

Pour mixture through a fine mesh sieve, placed over a bowl. Use a spoon to press out all the liquid and force through the sieve.

Store in a secure jar or bottle.

The Recipes

So, in the previous section you learned all the hot sauce recipes you can whip up.

But what good is a sauce if you have nothing to add it to?

That's what this section of the book is all about. Simple and delicious recipes using various homemade hot sauces.

So dive into this section and check out the range of breakfast, lunch and dinner recipes that all have a spicy twist to them.

All the sauces from the previous section will go as an amazing condiment with any meat, poultry or veggie dish so experiment a little bit and see what your favourite combination is.

Enjoy.

Breakfast

Sweet Potato Hashbrown

Ingredients: Serves 2

2 sweet potatoes
1 egg
2 teaspoon garlic salt
1 teaspoon olive oil
Salt
Homemade Sriracha

Directions

Pierce multiple holes in sweet potato with a fork and microwave on high for 5 minutes.

Once cooled, skin the potatoes and cut into 1cm cubes. If difficult to cut, microwave again for 3 minutes.

Take a medium pan, place over a medium heat and add the olive oil.

Sauté the potato cubes for 15 minutes. Halfway through add the garlic salt and toss to coat.

Once potatoes are browned and cooked, make a hole in the middle of them and cook the egg in this space.

Sprinkle with salt, to taste

Add homemade Sriracha sauce, to taste

Ingredients: Serves 2

Hollandaise sauce
12 tablespoons butter, unsalted
6 egg yolks
½ cup boiling water
2 teaspoons lemon juice
¼ teaspoon black pepper
¼ teaspoon garlic salt
¼ teaspoon sea salt
Homemade Sriracha sauce, to taste

Eggs benedict
2 poached eggs
2 English muffins, toasted and buttered
1 avocado, stoned and skin removed, thinly sliced
1 large tomato, finely sliced
½ cup shredded cheese
Sea salt
Black pepper

Directions

To make hollandaise sauce:

Add 2 cups of water to a pot and bring to the boil, turn heat down. Place a heatproof bowl over the simmering water and whisk the butter and egg yolks together.

Slowly and carefully add the ½ cup of boiling water to the mixture, whisking continually.

Continue to whisk slowly, increase the temperature on the pot containing the water. Heat the mixture until it is thickened, should take around 8-10 minutes.

Remove from the heat.

Whisk in the lemon juice, black pepper, garlic salt, sea salt, and Sriracha to taste.

Serve warm.

To assemble:

Add cheese to toasted English muffin. Layer with tomato, avocado, and then the poached eggs.

Drizzle the sauce over everything.

Salt and pepper to taste.

Veggie Frittata

Ingredients: Serves 4

6 eggs
Homemade Sriracha, to taste
2 tablespoons grated parmesan
¼ teaspoon black pepper
Pinch of salt
2 teaspoons olive oil
1 red onion, sliced
2 garlic cloves, minced
1 teaspoon parsley
1 cup chopped mushrooms
1 red bell pepper, chopped
1 cup spinach
⅓ crumbled goat's cheese

Directions

Turn grill/broiler to high.

Add eggs, Sriracha sauce, pepper and salt to a mixing bowl and whisk together.

Add olive oil to pan and place over medium heat. Add the garlic and onions, along with a pinch of salt, sauté for around 5 minutes.

Add bell peppers, mushrooms, parsley and cook for another 5 minutes. Add the spinach at the 4 minute mark and let wilt.

Add the egg mixture, stir a few times and allow to set.

Sprinkle the goat's cheese on top. Don't stir.

Transfer pan to the oven and leave for 5 minutes.

Serve and add more Sriracha to taste.

Devilled Cheese Toast

Ingredients: Serves 1-2

8 oz. cheddar, grated
¼ cup dill pickles, chopped
¼ cup mayonnaise
2 tablespoons chopped pimientos
4 thick cut slices bread, toasted
Homemade hot sauce (use your favourite), to taste
Salt and pepper, to taste

Directions

Preheat grill/broiler.

Toast bread under grill, turning half way

Take a large mixing bowl and mix together all ingredients.

Once bread is toasted spoon over the mixture on top and place back under the grill for 2 minutes.

Serve hot and add more hot sauce to taste.

Breakfast Tacos

Ingredients: Serves 4

6 oz. chorizo sausage, sliced or torn
8 medium sized corn tortillas
6 eggs
¼ cup milk
½ teaspoon pepper
½ teaspoon salt
1 cup shredded cheddar cheese
1 teaspoon homemade Tabasco sauce, or more to taste
½ cup medium salsa

Directions

Heat grill/broiler to medium-high heat.

Place a pan over a medium heat and add the chorizo.

Cook for 5 minutes or until browned all over. Remove chorizo and set aside.

Whisk together the eggs, milk, salt and pepper in a bowl. Pour into the pan you used for the chorizo.

Cook until almost firm then add the sausage and cook for a further minute. Stir continually. Take off the heat and let rest.

Place tortillas, even spread under the grill and toast for 30 seconds per side. They should be crispy on the edges but still pliable.
Remove tortillas from oven. Add egg and sausage mixture onto the tortillas, spoon some salsa and sprinkle cheese on top.

Season with more tabasco to taste.

Simple Spiced Omelette

Ingredients: Serves 1-2

4 whole eggs
½ cup milk
½ teaspoon garlic powder
1 teaspoon paprika
1 tablespoon olive oil
Your favourite homemade hot sauce
¼ cup medium salsa
¼ cup grated cheese
Handful of spinach leaves

Directions

Place a large pan over a medium heat and add the oil.

Whilst the oil heats, take a small bowl and whisk the eggs, garlic, paprika and milk together.

Pour the egg mixture into the pan and after 30 seconds turn down the heat to low.

Let cook for a few minutes, until the surface of the omelette begins to cook.

To one side only, add the spinach, salsa, cheese and hot sauce to taste.

Continue to cook for 1 minute, running your spatula around the rim of pan to loosen the egg.

Fold the empty half of the omelette over to the other side, enclosing the ingredients.

Take off the heat and leave for 1 minute.

If you want serve more hot sauce to taste.

Lunch

BBQ Chicken Sandwich

Ingredients: Serves 2

2 Chicken breasts, sliced lengthwise
3 garlic cloves, minced or finely chopped
3 tablespoons of paprika
2 red onions, thinly sliced
½ cups water
2 tablespoons oil
¼ grated cheddar cheese
Homemade BBQ sauce
2 rolls or thick sliced bread

Directions

Place a pan over a medium heat and add the olive oil.

Add the chicken, water, garlic, onion and paprika to the pan and cook until the chicken is cooked through. Stir frequently.

Once the chicken is cooked and the water has evaporated take off the heat and sprinkle the cheddar in. Add BBQ sauce to taste.

Stir until the chicken and onions are coated with the melted cheese.

Lump onto your bread or rolls and add more BBQ sauce if required. .

Glazed Salmon

Ingredients: Serves 4

½ cup apricot nectar
⅓ cup roughly chopped dried apricots
2 tablespoons honey
2 tablespoons soy sauce
1 tablespoon grated ginger, or powder
2 cloves garlic, minced, or finely chopped
Any homemade hot sauce, to taste
¼ teaspoon ground cinnamon
4 salmon fillets, skin removed

Directions

Preheat oven to 350F and oil a baking pan

Place a pan over a medium heat. Add the apricot nectar, apricots, honey, soy sauce, ginger, garlic, cinnamon and hot sauce. Mix together well in the pan.

Bring to a boil over the medium heat, once it starts simmering turn the heat to low and let it simmer, stirring occasionally, until reduced by half. Should take about 20 minutes.

Spoon out ¼ cup of the glaze for basting. Set the rest aside for now.

Put the salmon fillets on the oiled baking pan and brush with the glaze from the pan.

Bake in oven for 15-20 minutes or until salmon flakes easily with a fork.

Turn once during cooking at the halfway point.

Towards the end of cooking baste frequently with the ¼ cup of glaze you set aside.

Add more hot sauce to taste at end of cooking.

Serve with a green salad.

Black Bean & Salsa Soup

Ingredients: Serves 4

2 cans black beans, drained
½ cups vegetable broth
1 cup medium salsa
½ teaspoon ground cumin
4 tablespoons sour cream
2 green onions, thinly sliced
Roasted Tomatillo & Jalapeno Salsa Verde sauce, to taste

Directions

In a food processor add the beans, broth, salsa, cumin, tomatillo sauce and blend for 45-60 seconds (depending on how smooth you like your soup).

Pour the contents into a pan and heat over a medium heat until it begins to simmer. Turn heat to low and leave for 5 minutes.

Before serving top each bowl of soup with 1 tablespoon of the sour cream and sprinkle with green onion.

Give people the sauce bottle to let them adjust to their personal taste.

Slow Cooker Turkey Chili

Ingredients: Serves 6-8

1 tablespoon vegetable oil
1 pound ground turkey
2 cans of tomato soup
2 cans kidney beans, drained
1 can black beans, drained
1 medium onion, chopped
4 tablespoons your favourite hot sauce
½ tablespoon garlic, minced or powder
Ground black pepper
1 teaspoon ground allspice
Salt to taste

Directions

Take a pan and place over a medium heat. Add the oil and warm. Add the ground turkey and cook until evenly brown all over. Drain off any liquid or fat.

Add the turkey, tomato soup, beans and chopped onion to your slow cooker. Season with pepper, allspice, garlic and hot sauce to taste.

Cover and cook for 8 hours at a low setting.

Fish Tacos

Ingredients: Serves 6

Marinade
¼ cup olive oil
2 tablespoons white vinegar
2 tablespoons lime juice, fresh is best
Zest of half a lime
1.5 teaspoons honey
2 cloves garlic, minced or finely chopped
½ teaspoon cumin
1/2 teaspoon chili powder
1 teaspoon seafood seasoning, any store bought brand
Ground black pepper, to taste
Homemade hot sauce, to taste
1 pound tilapia fillets, cut into chunks

Sauce
1 cup sour cream
2 tablespoons lime juice, fresh is best
Zest of half a lime
¼ teaspoon cumin
¼ teaspoon chili powder
½ teaspoon seafood seasoning, any store bought brand
Salt and pepper to taste

Other
1 pack of tortillas
3 medium tomatoes, seeded and diced
1 bunch of cilantro, coarsely chopped
2 limes, cut in wedges

Directions

For Marinade:

Put all the ingredients, except the fish, in a bowl and mix them well.

Lay fish in a shallow bowl and pour the marinade over it.

Cover and place in the refrigerator for 6 hours.

For Sauce:

In a bowl add the sour cream, adobo sauce and mix well. Stir in the lime juice, zest, cumin, chili powder and seafood seasoning. Salt and pepper to taste and stir well again.

Cover and refrigerate.

To Cook:

Take a pan and place over a medium heat. Add a splash of oil and warm.

Add the fish along with any remaining marinade and cook until the fish is easy to flake with a fork. Should be 10-15 minutes. Be sure to flip the fish to avoid it sticking to pan.

Once it is easy to flake with a fork, turn off the heat and begin to break the fish up in the pan using a spatula.

In a bowl toss the tomatoes and cilantro in homemade hot sauce.

Use three serving bowls. 1 is for the sauce, 1 is for the cooked fish, 1 is for the spicy tomato and cilantro mix.

Let people assemble their own tacos with the tortillas.

Ingredients: Serves 2

1 can of tuna
1 egg
⅔ cup quick-cooking oats
3 tablespoons homemade BBQ sauce, use either one
3 tablespoons finely chopped green onion
1 teaspoon homemade hot sauce, or to taste
½ teaspoon dried savory
Salt, one pinch
1 tablespoon oil

Directions

Take a bowl and add the tuna, eggs and oats, mix until blended together.

Add the BBQ sauce, green onion, hot sauce, savory and the salt. Stir well.

Place a pan over a medium heat add the oil. Once warmed spoon the tuna mix into the pan and flatten slightly. Smaller is better for this as they will hold form easier.

Cook until browned on each side. Should take around 3-4 minutes per side.

Serve up with a side salad.

Veggie Chickpea Filling

This is great for wraps, sandwiches and panini's. So take your pick.

Ingredients: Serves 1-2

1 can of chickpeas, drained and rinsed
1 stalk of celery, coarsely chopped
½ onion, finely chopped
1 tablespoon mayonnaise
1 tablespoon lemon juice
Any of the homemade sauces from this book
Salt and pepper, to taste

Directions

In a large bowl add all ingredients and mix well. Use a fork to flatten some of the chickpeas.

Season to taste

Simple as that.

Dinner

Duck & Pak Choi Salad

Ingredients: Serves 1-2

1 Duck breast
2 medium sweet potatoes
Pack of pak choi salad, or pak choi leaves
Sesame Seeds
1 tablespoon olive oil
Homemade blackberry BBQ sauce, to taste

Directions

Pierce sweet potatoes multiple times and microwave on a plate for 10 minutes.

Cut in half, pierce the inside surfaces and microwave for a further 5 minutes.

Let cool, skin the potatoes and roughly chop. Add to bowl and mash either with a fork, spatula or your hands. Set aside.

Place a pan over a medium heat and add olive oil. Once heated add the duck breast, skin side down.

Add 2 tablespoons of BBQ sauce, flip the breast and continue to cook. Duck can, and should, be served pink in the middle so don't worry too much about cooking times.

With two minutes of cooking time to go add the pak choi and sesame seeds to the pan and allow them to soak and cook in the juices of the duck.

Take off the heat, add 1 tablespoon of BBQ sauce and set aside to rest.

Microwave the sweet potato mash to reheat.

Serve as follows. Bed of pak choi, mound of sweet potato mash, duck breast on top.

Drizzle anything left in the pan over the dish.

Lime & Sriracha Chicken

Ingredients: Serves 4

6 boneless chicken thighs, or 4 halved chicken breasts
¼ cup extra virgin olive oil
Juice of 1 lime
½ large onion, sliced
1 tablespoon homemade Sriracha, or more to taste
Chopped cilantro for garnish

Directions

Preheat oven to 400F

Season the chicken with salt & pepper. Rub in using your hands.

Combine the oil, lime juice, Sriracha, onion and chicken in a bowl and toss well to coat. Cover and refrigerate for 1-2 hours.

Add chicken to an oven proof bowl and pour the marinade atop.

Cook for 25 minutes before switching to grill/broil and cooking until the tops brown.

Remove from oven and garnish with more Sriracha and the chopped cilantro

Cajun Scallops

Ingredients: Serves 2

1 teaspoon olive oil
1 red onion, thinly sliced, separated into rings
1 teaspoon Cajun powder
½ teaspoon ground black pepper
1 teaspoon butter, unsalted
1 garlic clove, minced or chopped finely
3 - 4 pounds fresh scallops
1 teaspoons habanero hot sauce, or more if you like it spicy

Directions

Take a pan and place over a high heat, add the oil and heat for 15 seconds.

Add the onions, seasoning and pepper. Cook for 2 minutes. Add the butter and garlic and cook for a further 30 seconds.

Add the scallops and cook for 1 minute each side (should be well browned). Drizzle with hot sauce as you cook.

Cook for 3 minutes.

Thai Garlic Vegetarian Stir Fry

Ingredients: Serves 3-4

1 bag of bean sprouts
1 carrot, shredded
1 red onion, finely sliced
½ white onion, finely sliced
2 bell peppers, deseeded and chopped
½ courgette chopped
¼ cup pumpkin seeds
2 tablespoons oil
Homemade Thai chili sauce, to taste

Directions

Place a wok over a high heat and add the olive oil.

Add the carrot, onions, peppers, courgette and cook on high for 4 minutes. Stirring frequently

Lower the heat to medium and add the bean sprouts, Thai chilli sauce and cook for 5 minutes. Stirring frequently

Take off the heat and add the pumpkin seeds, stir well.

Leave to sit for 2 minutes.

Serve and season to taste.

Beef Skewers in a Habanero Nut Sauce

Ingredients: Serves 4

For the meat
½ cup finely diced onion
3 cloves garlic, minced, or finely chopped
1 tablespoon grated ginger, or powder
1 teaspoon brown sugar
2 teaspoons homemade Sriracha sauce
1 tablespoon finely chopped cilantro
¼ cup soy sauce
2 teaspoons sesame oil
Juice of 1 lime
1.5 pounds skirt steak cut into ½ inch thick slices
Bamboo skewers, pre-soaked in water

For the habanero nut sauce
1 cup smooth peanut butter
½ cup hot water
2 cloves garlic, minced
2 tablespoons soy sauce
1 teaspoon cumin
1 teaspoon habanero sauce
½ teaspoon curry powder
Juice of 1 lime

Directions

To make the marinade:

Add the chopped onion, garlic, ginger and sugar to a re-sealable bag. Add the red chili paste, cilantro, soy sauce, sesame oil and lime to juice to the bag and seal.

Massage the bag to mix well.

Add the beef strips to the bag and marinate for 6 hours.

Preheat grill/broiler to high.

Skewer the beef onto the skewers and grill for 6 minutes, turning frequently. Baste with the marinade every minute.

Serve with the Habanero nut sauce.

To make sauce:

Mix all ingredients together and beat until smooth, adding 2 tablespoons extra of water if necessary.

Peri-Peri Chicken

Ingredients: Serves 4

1 whole chicken
Homemade peri-peri sauce
Salt and Pepper

Directions

Pour sauce over chicken, sprinkle with salt and pepper. Using your hands rub the chicken to ensure it is coated well.

Place chicken in container and cover. Refrigerate for 8-24 hours.

Preheat oven to 390F.

Roast the chicken according to instructions on the wrapping that the chicken came in.

Before serve drizzle more peri-peri sauce over.

Serve with chips and salad.

Gumbo

Ingredients: Serves 4-6

1 pound Andouille sausage, cut into chunks
4 chicken breasts, cut into chunks
Vegetable oil
¾ cup flour, all-purpose
1 onion, finely sliced
½ bell pepper, deseeded and chopped
2 celery ribs, sliced
8 cups hot water
3 garlic cloves, minced
1.5 tablespoons Worcestershire sauce
2 teaspoons Creole seasoning
½ teaspoons dried thyme
1 teaspoon homemade hot sauce, choose whichever you like
Cooked white grain rice
4 chopped green onions

Directions

Place a pan over a medium heat, with a splash of olive oil and add the chopped sausage. Cook for 5 minutes, stirring frequently.

Remove sausage from pan and set aside.

Cook the chicken in the oil left over by the sausage for 5 minutes, or until browned on all sides. Ensure you stir frequently.

Remove chicken and set aside.

Add a gulp of oil. Add the flour and cook over a medium heat for 20-25 minutes. Stirring constantly. It will become chocolate coloured after this time.

Add the onion, bell pepper, celery and cook for 10 minutes, or until they are tender.

Add the water and slowly and bring the mixture to the boil. Add the chicken, garlic and next 5 ingredients to the pan and reduce the heat to low. Let simmer for 30 minutes.

Add the sausage and chopped green onion to the gumbo. Let simmer for 20 minutes, stirring occasionally.

Serve over hot rice.

Garnish with more hot sauce to taste.

BBQ Shrimp

Ingredients: Serves 6-8

4 pounds of large shrimp, unpeeled
½ cup butter, unsalted is best
½ cup olive oil
¼ cup chili sauce
¼ cup Worcestershire sauce
2 lemons, sliced
4 garlic cloves, finely chopped
2 tablespoons creole seasoning
2 tablespoons lemon juice
1 tablespoon chopped parsley
1 teaspoon paprika
1 teaspoon oregano
1 teaspoon ground red pepper
Homemade BBQ sauce, to taste
.

Directions

In a pan, over a medium heat, add the butter and the remaining ingredients. Cook for 3 minutes, stirring continually.

On a baking tray, spread a sheet of aluminium foil. Lay the shrimp on this.

Pour the sauce over the shrimp and cover. Leave covered for 60 minutes, turning once during this time.

Preheat oven to 400F

Remove the cover and bake for 20 minutes.

Serve along side bread or on a bed of noodles.

BBQ Sirloin Steaks

Ingredients: Serves 2

2 Sirloin steaks
2 garlic cloves, chopped
1 red onion, sliced
3 tablespoons olive oil
Meat speciality BBQ sauce
Salt and pepper
Salad leaves
2 tablespoons balsamic vinegar

Directions

Season steaks with BBQ sauce, salt and pepper. Rub into the meat and leave for 15 minutes at room temperature.

Put a pan over a medium heat and add 2 tablespoons olive oil. Toss in the onion and garlic in the pan, cook for 5 minutes.

Add remaining oil and turn heat to high. Push onions and garlics to edge of pan away from the centre.

Once pan is sizzling hot add steaks and cook to your liking.

Once cooked, take off the heat and let steak rest for 4 minutes. Move onions back towards the steak and let them absorb the juices.

In a bowl add the salad leaves and balsamic vinegar. Toss to coat leaves.

Serve salad on side of steak.

Habanero Salsa Tacos

Ingredients: Serves 2

5 chicken thighs, boneless
Skin of 5 chicken thighs (see above ingredient)
Homemade habanero hot sauce
4 green onions, chopped finely
¼ cup chopped cilantro
2 large tomatoes, deseeded and chopped
3 tablespoons lemon juice
¼ small head of iceberg lettuce
1 avocado, stone removed, peeled, and chopped
4 tortillas
Salt and pepper
2 tablespoons olive oil

Directions

Preheat oven to 350F.

Add the skinned chicken thighs to a baking tray lined with foil and season with salt and pepper. Cook the chicken thighs for 30 minutes, until cooked through.

Remove from oven, let cool and shred when cool enough to touch.

Place a pan over a low-medium heat and add 1 tablespoon oil. Lay the chicken skin, fat side down, and let crisp. If air pockets develop just press them down with a spoon.

Cook for 6 minutes before turning. Salt them.

Whilst the skins cook, put the green onions, cilantro, tomatoes, lemon juice and habanero sauce into a food processor. Blend for 15 seconds to combine. Set aside.

Once the chicken skins are well browned and crisp take them from the pan and cut into strips.

Drain any fat from the pan and add the remaining oil. Cook the tortillas, one at a time in the pan removing after 20 seconds. Heat should be medium and ensure you turn once.

In a bowl add the tomatoes, lettuce, cilantro, onion and habanero sauce (to taste). Toss well and season with salt and pepper.

Assemble the tacos using the habanero salsa, shredded chicken and chicken skin strips.

Serve hot or cold.

Sriracha Chicken Burgers

Ingredients: Serves 2-4

2 pounds of ground chicken
1 packet ranch salad dressing and seasoning mix, any store should have this
4 burger buns or rolls
1 large tomatoes, sliced
Shredded lettuce
4 tablespoons mayonnaise
Sriracha, to taste
Salt and pepper, to taste

Directions

In a bowl mix together, using your hands, the ground chicken, small amount of Sriracha and ranch seasoning. Season with salt and pepper, mix well.

Form the chicken into 4 patties, don't press them together to hard.

Heat grill to medium and cook burgers. Grill until well done. Flipping occasionally.

Once cooked you just need to stack your burger buns. Add the lettuce, tomato and mayonnaise then place the chicken burger on top.

Add Sriracha to taste.

Enjoy this book?

Please leave a review and let others know what you liked about this book?

https://www.amazon.com/gp/css/order-history *and click on Digital Orders.*

Just click the link above and it will take you straight to your amazon account.

Reviews are so crucial to self-published authors like myself and it would mean the world to me if you could leave me a quick review. Even one sentence would make a huge difference to me!

Lots of Love,

Sarah Sophia

Made in the USA
San Bernardino, CA
02 February 2014